GW00392439

A Century of Stamford
Coachbuilding

PRIZE WAGONS AND CARTS.

HAYES AND SON,

SCOTGATE WORKS, STAMFORD,

Manufacturers to H.M. Board of Ordnance,  And all the Principal Railways in the Kingdom.

COACH AND CART WHEELWRIGHTS.

SPRING VAN AND WAGON BUILDERS.

TIMBER MERCHANTS, CONTRACTORS, &c.

MANUFACTURERS OF

Carts, Vans, Wagons, Trucks, and Implements,

 For Railways, Town Use, Agriculture, and Exportation.

CONTRACTORS' & BUILDERS'

Dobbin and other Carts, Barrows, &c.

A
CENTURY OF
STAMFORD
COACHBUILDING

A history of Henry Hayes and Son,
carriage and waggon builders of
Stamford, Peterborough and London
(1825-1924)

by

MICHAEL KEY

STAMFORD
Published by Paul Watkins
With the co-operation of Lincolnshire County Council:
Stamford Museum
1990

Published by

Paul Watkins

18, Adelaide Street,

Stamford, Lincolnshire, PE9 2EN.

Photoset by Paul Watkins (Publishing)

from the disk of Michael Key

ISBN

1 871615 74 7

Acknowledgements

It is not possible to acknowledge individually the many people who have helped with the research into Hayes and Son. They include co-members of the Stamford Survey Group, in particular the late John H. Chandler, the staff at Stamford Town Hall, Stamford Museum, Stamford Library and the R.A.S.E. Library; David Roffe for help with editing the text and Martin Smith for drawing the maps. Also the local people who have shared their memories with me. And there are also those members of the Hayes family with whom chance has brought me into contact, especially Peggy Hayes, Joyce Buck and the late Barbara Hayes. The interest they have shown has encouraged me to complete as far as it is possible this history. I hope they find this chapter in their family's history as interesting to read as I found it to research.

Printed and bound by Woolnoughs of Irthlingborough

Contents

List of plates

Introduction

Across one of the entrances to the Fire Station in Radcliffe Road, Stamford, stands a pair of green painted gates made from two iron wheels. Not so unusual perhaps, and admittedly they are rather plain and ordinary. But take a closer look, see the name proudly cast in the iron hubs, 'HENRY HAYES AND SON STAMFORD.' This pair of gates is one of the last memorials to a firm of carriage and waggon builders whose reputation for craftsmanship of the highest order spanned almost one hundred years (Plate 2).

It was not merely a provincial reputation either. From their works came elegant and luxurious carriages for the Prince of Wales, the King of Sweden and the Gaekwar of Baroda. There was a steady stream of almost every conceivable type of horse-drawn vehicle; from dainty little dog carts to iron carts for the disposal of night soil; and robust carts and waggons for railway contractors and for military campaigns. Their carriages and carts were to be found in Capetown and Tasmania: their wheelbarrows in China. They even had an early, though brief, flirtation with the internal combustion engine.

Hayes and Son were makers of vehicles which were not only robust and sturdy, but were of 'good style and appearance.' They began building carts and waggons when the stage coach was still at its peak and continued until the motor car was a common sight on the roads. A large number of their customers were brewers: Phillips' and Hunt's breweries in Stamford thought Hayes produced 'excellent vehicles ... substantially built'; more than twenty vehicles were supplied to Lichfield Brewery and fourteen of various kinds were sent to Richard Warwick and Sons of Newark on Trent. Mr R.H.Ming of the Nine Elms depot of the London and South Western Railway Company wrote in 1879 that the "great number of vehicles of every description ... supplied to this company during the past twenty years, have given every satisfaction, hence our continued and uninterrupted use of your vehicles." Hayes also received a letter of satisfaction from J. C. Wombwell of Wombwell's Menagerie on the receipt of a Rhinoceros Waggon.[1]

The Beginning (1825)

Henry Hayes was born in 1798 at Stibbington, a small village on the old Great North Road, in what is now Cambridgeshire. His father Richard was the village carpenter. It is probable that he was descended from the papermaking family of Hayes who ran the paper mills at Stibbington and nearby Southwick. By 1820 Henry had married and in 1825 set up as a wheelwright on his own account. His workshop was probably in the neighbouring village of Wansford where in 1821 his only son, John, was born. When Henry moved to Stamford is not known. He first appears in the Stamford Directories in 1842 as a wheelwright in Scotgate but it is clear that he had been working in the town for at least seven years before because in 1835 his fourteen year old son John became his apprentice and the indenture describes Henry as 'wheelwright of St John's parish.' When John later became a freeman of the Borough of Stamford by virtue of his being the son of a freeman a further clue to Henry's arrival in the town can be uncovered. The Stamford freemen's Registers show a Henry Hayes having purchased his freedom on 9 October 1834, as a victualler in Castle Street. This Henry Hayes was listed as a £10 voter in Castle Street from 1832 until 1838, but after this date the series is incomplete. The *Stamford Mercury* for 11 March 1831 tells us that 'Mr Hayes' was landlord of the Shepherd and Shepherdess in Castle Street (now number 5), while the 1830 Poll Book takes us back to the earliest entry for Henry. It is not unusual for a tradesman also to be a publican (there are several examples to be found in the town) and Henry may have needed a second income to support himself and his family while he built up his wheelwrighting business. Why Henry came to Stamford can only be a matter of speculation. There were a number of Hayes living in the town to whom he may have been related, but more importantly, there would have been more opportunities for an energetic young man in a small, bustling market town than in a sleepy little village.

There is some uncertainty as to where in Stamford Henry set up his new workshop. At the time of his death in 1871 he was living in a house on the corner of Scotgate and West Street, but there is no evidence to suggest that this was ever more than just a dwelling. The house was demolished in 1872 to make way for the extension of St John's school. The most likely site for Henry's workshop is at 69-70, Scotgate and behind 16, All Saints Place which had been developed for industry by the early nineteenth century. It was probably here that John Hames (who owned 70-73 Scotgate and who built 16, All Saints Place) and later his son

John jnr. had a builders' yard and workshops. This business came to an end with the death of John Hames jnr. in 1828 and it is probable that Henry Hayes was then able to take over the yard. Newcombe's 1862 Stamford Directory places Hayes and Son at 'Scotgate Works, All Saints Place.' Coincidentally Henry's grandson, Albert Henry, died at 16, All Saints Place in 1910. [2] (See map 1.)

On completion of his apprenticeship in 1842 John Hayes joined his father in the business and thus began a partnership which was to bring about the success of the firm. There is no doubt that John was the dominant partner and that his was the guiding hand. As the daughter of one of his later employees put it, "for John, things had to be just right, there were no half measures." At the age of twenty-four John married Maria Edey, the daughter of a Barnack blacksmith, who bore him three boys and three girls. Two other babies died in infancy. John was destined to outlive Maria and all three of his sons and to reach the age of ninety-four.

Growth (1850-1860)

By 1854 the reputation of Hayes and Son was well established. In that year they became one of the first waggon builders to gain a government contract when they supplied a number of waggons to H.M. Board of Ordnance for the Crimean War. Towards the end of the same year they received an order from the Great Northern Railway Company for eighty road coal vans. According to a report in the *Stamford Mercury* this was not the first time Hayes had won such an order from the G.N.R. "...the [G.N.R.] directors having several times given them preference, though the prices tendered were not the lowest." The same report goes on to say that "the light draught and durability of the Stamford vans and trolleys have now acquired a very extensive fame." To cope with this amount of work

Map showing location of Hayes' works in Stamford

8

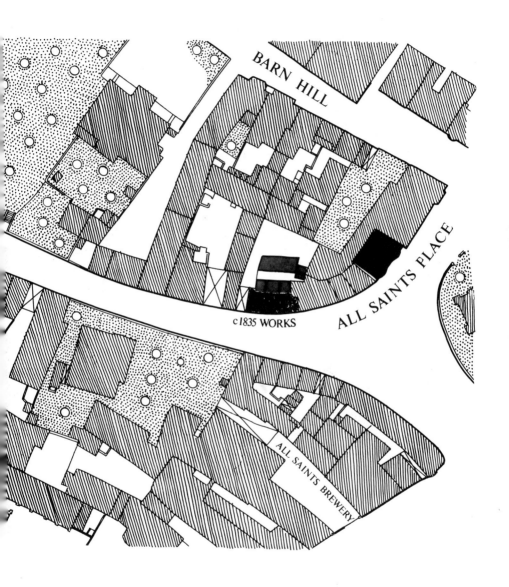

BARN HILL

ALL SAINTS PLACE

c 1835 WORKS

ALL SAINTS BREWERY

Hayes advertised in that year for six wheelwrights and two blacksmiths and promised them constant employment at new work. [3]

Hayes were believers in the importance of publicity and of showing off their products. The connection of Stamford to the growing railway network, to the Midland in March 1848 and to the Great Northern in November 1856, gave Hayes the opportunity to reach potential customers all over the country. In 1855 they attended a Royal Agricultural Society of England (R.A.S.E) exhibition for the first time. This annual showcase for the industry was then held at a different venue each year, often coinciding with other county shows. However, the problems of conflicting show dates seem not to have worried Hayes. They became regular exhibitors at many shows and exhibitions throughout the country during the next fifty years or so.

Three vehicles were sent to their first R.A.S.E. exhibition which was at Carlisle. Of these the first was an Improved Harvest Cart which had the

"great advantage in being low, and easily loaded, the body is 10ft long and 6ft wide - with a screw apparatus so as to adjust the weight on the horse's back when going down hill, or up, as it may be required, with the greatest of ease; mounted on four wheels and Scotch iron axle tree, it is so arranged that the wheels and the axle tree can be removed when required for the harvest and put under a manure cart body."

The cost of this cart was £15.15s.0d. with adjusting apparatus; £13 without. The second vehicle was a one or two horse Scotch Cart made "to suit all requirements of farm or road work - body made of well seasoned oak, and fitted with four inch wheels." It was priced at £14. At the Salisbury exhibition in 1857 this cart was to receive the first of hundreds of awards and commendations won by Hayes for the quality of their work. [4]

The last of the trio sent to Carlisle was the substantial, and more costly, Light Spring Lorrie or Dray priced at £30. It was "particularly suited for the use of railway carriers, merchants, maltsters etc, - fitted with patent axles and oil boxes - the exhibitors have a great demand for them throughout England and Scotland." This was the vehicle so successfully sold to the G.N.R. The following year (1858), Hayes added a Light Spring Pair Horse Waggon to their range. These four vehicles in both single and pair horse versions were to be displayed and sold all over the country for many years.

Not all production was devoted to carts and waggons at this time. In 1858 Hayes were commissioned by the Government to supply Stable

Map showing location of Hayes'
works in Peterborough

Barrows. When the contract ended in 1861 a staggering 4,000 barrows had been delivered. The contract was renewed for a further three years. Barrow making appears to have been a lucrative business, for in 1859 Hayes received an order to send 2,000 Entrenching Barrows to China. [5]

Hayes and Son exhibited at many agricultural shows around the country, the R.A.S.E. shows at Plymouth in 1863 and Manchester in 1869 being typical. At Plymouth Hayes won the first of their many cash prizes. The judges agreed that both the single and pair horse Tipping Carts which had been introduced the previous year were in the 'front rank' and awarded them both a prize of £4.10s.0d. Made with oak frames and elm plank sides, each cart had iron axle trees and patent iron stocks. The one horse cart had raves and loose side boards; on the pair horse cart these were fixed, but it also had removeable harvest ladders front and rear. The price for these two vehicles was £14 and £15.15s.0d. respectively. Also at Plymouth Hayes showed a most elegant pair horse Waggon. The £10 first prize went to this vehicle and no better description can be given than that in the judge's report.

> "...to Messrs Hayes and Son the whole of the money, 10*l.*, for their light, well made waggon, with a wide roomy body, constructed with a strong foundation of English oak and elm plank sides and fitted with fixed side boards. It has a curved head and tail ladders for carrying loose hay and corn, easily removed when not required. The front wheels back under the body, and the waggon turns in the room it stands upon. The hind wheels are large, and the construction ensures lightness of draught. A powerful break [*sic*] can be applied to both hind wheels without stopping the horses. Price complete. 30*l.*10*s.*"

If Plymouth was successful from Hayes' point of view, winning four cash prizes, the Manchester show four years later was even more of a triumph. The R.A.S.E. judges decided that as so many high quality vehicles were on show, each waggon should be tested against a dynamometer. In previous years they had tested steam engines and reaping and mowing machines in this way to measure efficiency to a common standard, but this was the first time horse-drawn vehicles had been so tested.

Each cart and single horse waggon was loaded with two tons of pig iron divided equally and placed centrally over the front and rear axles. The pair horse waggons were loaded with four tons of iron similarly distributed. They were then pulled along a prescribed length of road by a steam engine against the dynamometer. The outcome was a long and very detailed table of results which was later published in the R.A.S.E. journal. Five waggons were chosen for the four-ton test, and "a more splendid collection of really substantial and well built waggons were never placed together." Once again it is approriate to use the judge's words to describe the Hayes vehicles:

"Hayes won the first prize in this class; better workmanship than it [the pair horse waggon] exhibited could not possibly be seen. This waggon is very strongly built, of solid elm plank sides 1¾ inch thick, frame entirely of English oak, very strong, fitted with double shafts, fixed side boards, well ironed, with loose side and end boards for carrying manure; head and tail ladders well secured with body boards of elm, 1 inch thick, fitted with double break of 2¼ x ⅝ iron (passing under the body, and giving additional strength to the waggon); it is quick, powerful, and easy in action. The wheels are very strong and well made, with 3 x 7 tyre, axle 3 inches square (short), and secured by a strong plate of ½ inch iron underneath; price 35*l.*"

The judges were equally generous in their comments on the carts. They found the 'tilting apparatus' to be "the most simple, useful and effective." To Hayes' single horse cart they awarded the first prize of £8. It was, they said,

"very strongly built, of the same excellent workmanship he exhibited in his waggons; sides of solid elm planking 1¾ inch thick, strongly ironed; with head and tail ladders complete; tipping apparatus excellent, the part at all likely to get out of order could be renewed at minimal expense; through axle 2¾ inches square, wheels well made with 4 inches by ¾ inch tyre, the body carried on each side upon an iron flange of 6½ inches wide and ⅞ thick, part and parcel of the axle; body boards of elm an inch thick, placed lengthways; price 14*l.*10*s.*"

The judges were also impressed by the two horse cart and it too was awarded the £8 first prize. A fourth first prize was received by Hayes for their Harvest Cart which was awarded £10. It was described by the judges as

"a substantial, yet light cart, the body low and entirely of ash, upon a frame 4 inches square; sides strengthened by iron spindles of ¼ inch round rod, placed at equal distances of 6 inches. lined with willow boards of ⅜ inch thick, iron axle through, of 4 x ⅝ inch; wheels 4 feet 10 inch, tyre 4 x ⅜ in. length of body 9 feet 10 inches; width 4 feet 4 inches; head and tail rails projecting two feet. The wheels are protected from interfering with the corn by an iron frame of ¾ inch thick, covered with a sheet of iron, of ⅛ inch by 10¼ inch broad, which is bolted to the cross pieces of the body, giving extra strength to the cart; price 15*l.*"

For Hayes and Son the Manchester show was a great success. In addition to their four first prizes they also took second prize for the two horse waggon and a commendation for a Light Spring Dray or Lorrie. Against competition from the larger manufacturers such as the Beverley

13

Waggon and Iron Co., the Bristol Waggon Co., and W. T. Crosskill they had almost scooped the pool. Obviously very satisfying.

Expansion (1860-1880)

Success, however, brought with it a problem: space, or rather a lack of it. The Scotgate Works had by the middle 1860s become very cramped. To provide much needed room for expansion John Hayes bought the New Road works of Peterborough coachmaker Abraham Allen in March 1866.[6] This 1200 sq yd site (which was actually in Chapel Street and has long since been redeveloped) included blacksmith's shops as well as wheelwright's shops. It not only gave John Hayes the space he needed but also the opportunity to enter the lucrative carriage building trade. This he did, with Abraham Allen's experience in the trade and with 'Mr Hayes jnr' superintending. Young Mr Hayes was probably John's eldest son Albert Henry. (See map 2.)

A further chance to expand came in 1869 when the long established firm Spencer's Coach Manufactory in Stamford High Street closed down. (See plate 4.) Founded about fifty years earlier by William Spencer, the business had been run since his retirement by his daughter Mary. Hayes bought the business in September 1869 and occupied the site until the middle 1880s.[7]

Hayes' first coach-built vehicle to be exhibited was an Aldershot Dog Cart shown at the R.A.S.E. Bury St Edmunds show in 1868. The following year at Leicester five carriages were on display including a Gentleman's Private Omnibus priced at £145. Hayes were catering for a somewhat different kind of customer than hitherto and from now on called themselves 'Coach and Carriage Builders.' Their range of coach-built vehicles rapidly expanded but the sturdy carts and waggons which had made them so successful would continue to be built alongside the more graceful products. Indeed, in 1868 a large number of carts were supplied for the Abyssinian expedition. During this period Hayes took on the lease of a site in West Street, Stamford, from the Borough Council, a move which was to prove most valuable in the future.

The wars of the 1870s brought in a great deal of work; during the Franco-Prussian war of 1870 a hundred waggons were built; in the 1877-78 Russo-Turkish war the entire works were put at the disposal of the Government and one hundred and fifty waggons produced. It took two months to build a transport cart, but several would be made simultaneously in an early form of mass unit construction.[8]

One of Hayes' more unusual orders came in 1870 from Alexander Fairgrieve, the proprietor of Wombwell's Menagerie. In July the Stamford Mercury reported that

> "Messrs Hayes and Son have just completed one of the largest and most attractive Velocipede Circuses yet constructed, - it carries upwards of fifty people and works in a circumference of 100 feet. The whole is conveyed in a very handsome van, built for the purpose, and was sent last week to Leeds fair."

Although nothing more is known about this machine, a photograph of another, smaller machine gives an idea of how it worked. It consisted of a circular track or railway to which was attached a ring of velocipedes (an early form of bicycle). These were propelled around the track by energetic customers with a great deal of merriment. It seems a strange form of enjoyment, to pay for the privilege of providing the motive power for the machine, but this was before the bicycle became an easily affordable means of transport. The machine owner had a brake to stop the riders after they had had their allotted time but this often became impossible to operate when a large group of lusty young men were determined to get their money's worth and they would go round and round until they tired of the sport.[9] (See plate 7.)

Hayes' connection with the travelling showmen was renewed in 1874 with an order from Edmonds' (Wombwell's) menagerie for a Rhinoceros waggon, the incumbent having possibly outgrown the one they built in 1869. It must have been a splendid vehicle, some 22 feet long, 9 feet wide and 11 feet high, weighing over four tons and richly decorated with carved and painted wood. It was divided into three compartments, one in the centre for the rhinoceros and on either side a cage for smaller animals. Because of its size carriage by rail was impractical so a team of eight of

Edmonds' horses were to drag it to Manchester where the menagerie was on show. The *Stamford Mercury* thought its "departure will no doubt be a sight." Unfortunately the paper failed to report the event.[10]

In 1871, on 18 March, Henry Hayes died aged seventy-three. He was a product of the industrial revolution; an enterprising craftsman who combined the skill of his hand with a shrewd business sense to develop his small town workshop into a major vehicle manufactory. His firm's products, made to his high standards of craftsmanship, were to be found in many overseas countries from Europe to New Zealand. The family firm, of which he must have been proud, was destined to grow even larger under the hand of his son John. The policy of exhibiting around the country continued and the range of vehicles was further expanded.

Hayes and Son's most impressive display of this period was at the great International Agricultural Exhibition held at Kilburn, London, in July 1879 where thirty-three vehicles were assembled. Included were all the prize winning carts and waggons, drays and vans; all in single or pair horse versions. Among the many carriages on the stand were a Brougham, a Stanhope Waggonette, a Lady's Phaeton, a Connaught Car and several types of Dog Cart. The prices ranged from £17 for a single-horse cart to £175 for a landau. At the very bottom of the price range was a collection of wheelbarrows, still worthy of a place in the catalogue. Brickmaker's Crowding Barrows and Bearing Off Barrows were £1.14s.0d. Excavator's Barrows were 12s.6d. The last, constructed of 'good seasoned material and a strong wheel', had been reduced in price since they were first introduced in 1875 at 14s.

Among the displays at the exhibition was a collection of 'Ancient and Modern Implements' which included some old farm carts and waggons. One waggon was reputed to be over two hundred years old. Another, an Oxford waggon made in 1786 and 'in regular daily use ever since' stood alongside a Hampshire waggon built in 1821. A pair of three horse carts were described as 'very clumsy and unwieldy' and 'very heavy.' Commenting on this display Hayes wrote in the catalogue: "By comparison, one of the old waggons stands unexcelled by our latest prize article, it is singular that so little if any progress should have been made by waggon manufacturers." A curious remark indeed, coming from one of the country's leading waggon builders.

Hayes put on another large display the same year at the R.A.S.E. Stamford show held in Burghley Park. Among the many exhibits to catch the eye of the *Stamford Mercury* reporter was a stylish Brougham Waggonette.

"...made with sliding glasses, with two lights in each side, and one in the door. The head is made to remove, and the back rests, with wings attached, are made to affix, thus forming an open carriage. It is very roomy, and must carry passengers in comfort, and is adapted for one or more pair of horses. The design throughout is very stylish, and the whole of the fittings are chaste and good. The painting is a rich ultramarine blue, relieved with lighter lines of blue, the trimming is of blue cloth, with silk laces to match; and the spring curtains, of which there is one to each window, are of crimson silk. It is also fitted with a powerful lever break [sic] to act upon both the hind wheels, an addition not often seen in the neighbourhood, but the carriage being built for a customer in Scotland, such appliances are absolutely necessary for the mountainous districts; and this one is especially commendable on account of the blocks being made to adapt themselves to the circumference of the wheels whenever applied."

So even if Hayes was unable to distinguish any progress in the designs of waggons, there were others able to appreciate the quality of his carriages and such innovations as the self adjusting brake.

Further Expansion (1880-1900)

The last two decades of the nineteenth century were years of growth and expansion. This may be seen by the extensive range of vehicles advertised; almost every trade or occupation was catered for. In what is believed to be the only existing Hayes document, an incomplete illustrated catalogue of 1880 (now in the Phillips' Collection, Stamford Town Hall), the firm claimed to produce three hundred vehicles annually. Whether this was true or merely advertiser's licence is unknown. What is clear is that a better organisation of the works was needed to cope with demand. So in 1880 John Hayes purchased the Rock Iron Works in Scotgate, Stamford, from George Snodin.

Rock Iron Works had been established in the late 1860s by agricultural implement makers John Coulson and Richard Wear. They produced straw elevators, threshing machines and a range of cultivating tackle. They also claimed to be steam engine inventors and manufacturers. During 1878 Coulson and Wear went into liquidation and sold the works to Snodin, a Nottingham engineer. Two years later Snodin moved his business to Albert Road in Stamford where he set up the Welland Iron Works trading as an agent for agricultural machinery and engines of all kinds.

Hayes bought the old iron works for £850 and set about rebuilding the site to suit his own purposes. The works backed onto premises in West Street which Hayes had been leasing from Stamford Borough Council since the 1860s. The purchase enabled the two sites to be integrated into one manufactory and the other Stamford premises to be closed.

A former public house alongside the iron works site, the Glaziers Arms, and the house next to it were demolished and a new showroom erected in their place. It was a stone and brick building, sixty feet long, with a Collyweston and blue slate roof. On the first floor were four workshops. Above the showroom windows Hayes fixed a large fleur de lis to advertise that the Prince of Wales was a customer; he had ordered a shooting brake at the 1878 Paris exhibition. Later, Hayes added the royal coat of arms although there is no record of any other royal patronage and both devices were fixed without permission, a common habit among enterprising Victorian businessmen.

At the rear of the showroom, across the yard, a stone-built blacksmiths' shop with a workshop and storeroom above was erected. Beside it was a large wheelwrights' shop, also built of stone. To pay for this work Hayes raised a mortgage of £1000. Thomas Perkins, an agricultural engineer from Hitchin, John Woods Sharman, a Wellingborough engineer, and Thomas White, a manufacturer from Bromsgrove, put up the money for which John Hayes agreed 4.5% per annum.[11]

Even the extra capacity which this new factory provided was not enough for John Hayes. He wanted to take advantage of the huge London market where the whole population seemed to be on wheels. Therefore in 1884 Hayes and Son took over and moved into 199/201 City Road, London, E, a building formerly occupied by Isaiah Abraham, Glass and Lead Merchant. Among the alterations required to improve the premises was the installation of a carriage lift to bring completed vehicles down from the first floor. Eight years later the toy factory of James Edwards at 197 City Road became vacant. Hayes also took over that building. Hayes may have owned these buildings but it is more likely that they were leased.[12]

Soon after this a Stamford directory entry in 1896 shows Hayes and Son to have a branch at 23, St Martin's High Street. These premises had long been associated with coach building, possibly the longest tenants being the Robertson family. John Robertson established his business here before 1800. After his death several members of the family ran the firm until 1872 when it was taken over by John Hibbins, a coachmaker who had worked for the Robertsons for thirty-seven years, and Thomas Paine, a coach trimmer (also a former employee; see plate 6.) An entry in the Burghley Estate water rate books suggests that Hayes probably acquired the business by 1894.[13]

New designs were continually being added to Hayes' already long catalogue during the 1880s and 90s. In 1884 they entered the dairy trade for the first time with the introduction of a milk van and a milk cart. Costing £30 and £21.10s.0d., they were awarded first prize by the British Dairy Farmers Association at the London Dairy Show of that year. In 1888 a milk barrow was offered at £10. Some years later a patent 'Hygienic Milk Tap' was available which ensured 'cleanliness and freedom from microbes,' priced 7s.6d.

A number of patented items and improvements to vehicles were advertised but whether any patents were held by Hayes has not been investigated. From 1881 carts and waggons were offered with or without Watling's Patent Tipping Gear, 'the easiest and the quickest' yet invented. At Lincoln in 1892 Hayes displayed a number of dog carts fitted with patent seats, the 'greatest improvement in pleasure dog carts ever introduced.' A modest declaration! In the following year when the Lincolnshire Agricultural Society exhibition was held at Stamford the Mayor, Mr F. Riley, bought one of the prize carts for £33. The cost seems a little high when compared to the £20 paid by Lazare Chaulduc of Baghdad. Perhaps it was fitted with patent seats.

Also on show was a delivery van built for the Anglo-American Oil Co. of London to be used for the carriage of paraffin. Hayes were later to build motor lorry bodies for this company (see plate 17). Also in 1893 John Hayes was introduced to the Gaekwar of Baroda. The outcome of this meeting was an order for a 'beautifully equipped brougham' to be delivered to India on completion.[14]

In December 1897 Hayes received an order from the British Government to supply twenty-five transport waggons. These were in addition to a recently completed order for fifty transport waggons and twenty-five forge carts. This was at a time when, following the first Boer War (1880-81), the British army was being strengthened. "The authorities at Woolwich are evidently alive to the importance of providing for future contingencies. When the War Office supplies the Volunteer force with transport (as soon it must) Hayes and Son will be even busier." The second Boer War was just two years away. "Owing to the intricacy of its details" a forge cart, for blacksmiths or farriers, took four months to make. They were made in pairs and were limbered together like gun-carriages. Forge carts were usually built in the Woolwich Arsenal but because of the urgency of the times Hayes, the government's oldest contractors, were given the job.[15]

Dispute and Decline (1900-1910)

If the last twenty years of the century saw an expansion of the firm, they also saw the beginning of its decline. As the nineteenth century drew towards its close, change was in the air for the carriage building industry, both in general and for Hayes in particular. The challenge of the internal combustion engine, then in its coughing and spluttering infancy, was something few carriage builders would be able to face successfully. Hayes and Son, like many other firms, tried to compete and adjust to the demands of the challenge but, like many other firms, would eventually succumb. However, the horseless carriage cannot be blamed entirely for the demise of the firm; the seeds of failure were sown internally, probably in the early 1890s.

By 1894 Albert Henry Hayes and John Eady Hayes, the eldest of John's sons, were partners in the business. The youngest son, William,

PRIZE WAGONS AND CARTS.

HAYES & SON,
SCOTGATE WORKS, STAMFORD,

Manufacturers to
H.M. Board of Ordnance,

and all the principal
Railways in the Kingdom.

COACH & CART WHEELWRIGHTS,
SPRING VAN AND WAGON BUILDERS,

TIMBER MERCHANTS, CONTRACTORS, &c.,

Manufacturers of

CARTS, VANS, WAGONS,
TRUCKS, AND IMPLEMENTS,

For Railways, Town use, Agriculture and Exportation, Contractors, and Builders.

DOBBIN & other CARTS, BARROWS, &c.

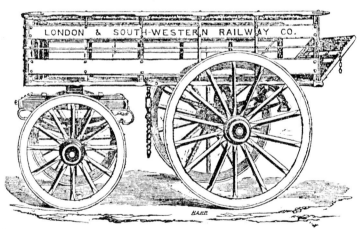

AN IMPROVED ONE-HORSE GOODS VAN,

Mounted upon Patent Axles, and fitted with 4 side and 3 cross Springs of best manufacture; front Wheels lock under. Body wide and square up, fitted with floating Raves, strengthened with angle Iron Plates, for top loading; the Framing of the Body made of best English Oak, and in every respect complete for Railway Carriers, Merchants, and Manufacturers, and very suitable for Town or Country.

2. These yard gates were removed from Hayes' Scotgate works when the building was demolished in 1967 and re-erected at the Radcliffe Road entrance to the Fire Station yard.

3. This Lowe, Son and Cobbold waggon photographed in their North Street, Stamford, yard is typical of the many such vehicles Hayes supplied to brewing firms all over the country.

4. This waggon by Hayes spent its working life on Flint's Farm, Belmesthorpe, and for a number of years was on display at Stamford Brewery Museum. Photographed at a Bourne saleroom in 1988. Stamford Museum.

5. A rare photograph of Spencer's Coach Manufactory, High Street, Stamford. It was demolished in the early 1960s. Stamford Museum.

5. Another rare picture, this time of Robertson's Coach Works in St Martins, taken in *c*.1874 soon after John Hibbins and Thomas Paine took over the business. Stamford Museum.

7. A Circus Velocipede. Unfortunately no photograph is known of the one built by Hayes for Alexander Fairgrieve but it was probably similar to this. Stamford Museum from an original in King's Lynn Museum.

6. John Hayes (1821-1916) during his first Mayoral year, 1884-85. Photograph given by Barbara Hayes.

9. These engravings of the Scotgate showrooms and the West Street works (drawn with considerable licence) are from Hayes' advertising material. They were found in a scrapbook in the Phillips Collection in Stamford Town Hall.

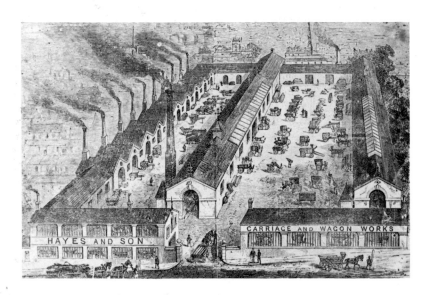

10. E. F. Young's town delivery van with its driver Mr Wade and his wife *c*.1900. A similar vehicle is now in The Museum of Lincolnshire Life, Lincoln. Photograph loaned by Andrew Jenkins.

11. Some of Hayes' work force display a selection of carriages outside the Scotgate showrooms *c*.1900. This was the Great North Road at its narrowest point.

12. J. H. Woodford's single-horse baker's cart at Barnack. Photograph loaned by Andrew Jenkins.

13. The Scotgate showrooms were featured on the firm's own postcard. This one, dated 15 January 1910, is addressed to 'The Coachman Walcote Hall Stamford.' The message reads "Dear Sir, If you are in Town on Monday with the Brougham: please call, so that we can try the Basket frame." One is intrigued to know whose is the motor car.

14. John Hayes photographed in November 1894 on the occasion of the presentation to him of a gold mounted walking stick and illuminated address to mark both his seventy-third birthday and his completion of a second term as Mayor. Photograph loaned by Joyce Buck.

15. Albert Henry Hayes (1846-1910) and his wife, Margaret (1851-1930), with their six sons *c.*1900. Standing from left: Percy (1886-1962), Maurice (1890-1967), William (1883-1932), John (1881-1961). Seated on left Henry (1885-1945), on right Noel (1888-1973). Photograph loaned by Peggy Hayes.

16. This aerial photograph of the Scotgate and West Street works was taken in 1938 soon after BXL Cascelloid Ltd had moved into West Street.

17. Leyland lorry bodied by Hayes at their Earl's Court Works for the Anglo-American Oil Co Ltd before the first World War.

18. The showroom in Scotgate just before demolition in 1967. Photograph by John C. Chandler.

19. Hayes and Son waggon wheel nut.

had died at the early age of twenty-five while working as his father's clerk. Albert, the eldest, took control of the firm when his father, now aged seventy-three, retired in 1894. John Eady joined the firm the same year. For some years he had been associated with the Stamford, Spalding and Boston Banking Company and probably brought with him considerable business expertise, which perhaps Albert was lacking. John took over the running of the London works while Albert ran the Stamford and Peterborough works. Some kind of conflict between the two seems to have developed. Whether it was at this time or later when John saw greater opportunities as his own master is not known. What is clear is that in 1901 he resigned his partnership and set up as a carriage builder under his own name at 132 East Road, just around the corner from Hayes' City Road works. This venture certainly seems to have been a success because the next year he acquired the City Road premises from Hayes and Son who then moved into 36 Carter Lane at the rear of St. Paul's Choir School. By 1903 John had moved out of London and was advertising his works at Kingsbury, St Albans and was able to mount a display of twenty-one vehicles at the R.A.S.E. Park Royal show.[16]

If there had been no dispute between the brothers earlier, there certainly was in 1903. An argument flared up over the exploitation by John of prizes awarded and recommendations received in the past by his brother's firm. He had given an undertaking in June not to use these awards in his advertising without making it clear that they had been gained by the firm of Hayes and Son and not by him or by his firm. Albert personally applied through the courts for a writ of attachment against John for alleged breaches of the undertaking. At the hearing, however, the judge refused the application and ordered that the two should come to a private agreement. It was agreed that John should pay £50 of Albert's costs on the understanding that he, Albert, would not press for a further order. Presumably John also agreed to honour the original undertaking. In the event no further action was to be needed, because John died suddenly in April 1904. Although John's death brought the argument to an end, it caused much bitterness between the two sides of the family for a long time afterwards. Until her own death in 1986, John's granddaughter, Barbara, was convinced that it was the court action which caused her grandfather's early death.[17]

Despite this internal wrangling and the disposal of the City Road works Hayes' varied production went on. In 1902 'Lord' George Sanger, the circus proprietor, commissioned the firm to build a miniature dress landau which was to be presented by the Van Dwellers' Association and

21

the Showmen of the United Kingdom to the children of the Prince and Princess of Wales. On completion in June it was put on display at the Scotgate showroom. Described as in the 'Queen Anne style' it was finished in lake colour lined out in red with dark blue upholstery, trimmed with dark blue lace and relieved by red piping. The wheels were rubber tyred. Hayes also made a set of silver mounted harness for the pair of skewbald red and cream ponies which were to draw the little carriage. This "dainty little vehicle, worthy of Cinderella herself, reflected the highest credit upon the artistic work of the firm." No doubt it brought a lot of pleasure to the royal children at Marlborough House. Fortunately this miniature landau survives and may be seen at the Royal Mews in London.[18]

By the turn of the century the influence of the internal combustion engine was beginning to have an effect on the carriage and waggon building industry. Many of the long established firms were turning to making motor car bodies, and Hayes were no exception. After all, the manufacturing techniques were much the same for horse-less carriages as they were for horse-drawn carriages. John Hayes snr. is reputed to have believed that "motor cars won't catch on," but despite this the firm made an entry into motor vehicle production in 1903.

Among the twenty vehicles on their stand at the R.A.S.E. show in Park Royal, London, that year was a self propelled van, "for the advertisement and delivery of goods - driven by a patent balanced engine through patent ratio gear contained in one tight case." The price in 1903 was £275. In 1904 and 1905 the price went up to £400. How many vehicles were made is not known, although it was reported that Hayes were

"meeting encouraging success with their motor vans. This firm are not buying the chassis and merely adding the body, but build the car throughout, having added greatly to their works for this purpose. The design of the engine is different from the standard pattern so rapidly getting stereotyped, and together with the change speed and differential gearing is simplicity itself. There are two speeds, forward and reverse."[19]

To discover that Hayes produced a motor vehicle is yet another lost aspect of the firm which evokes more questions than there are answers. Were they in fact making their own engines and chassis? It is doubtful if they had either the expertise or the finance for such a venture. So if they did not, who did make them and in what quantity? Far from expanding their works Hayes were shrinking. The City Road premises had gone to J. E. Hayes in 1902; in about 1903 or 1904 the Peterborough works were leased to coachbuilders Lawrence and Co. In 1906 the New Pick Motor Company took over the St Martins works in Stamford. Did Pick produce the engines and chassis? There is no answer yet. The London branch made another move in 1906, this time to Little Bridge Mews, Seagrave Road, Earl's Court where they made lorry bodies until it was closed down sometime in 1922.

Closure (1924)

The end of the firm was brought a little nearer in 1910 when Albert Henry Hayes died. He was sixty-four and had been an invalid for the past three years. Unlike his father he had never taken an active part in public affairs, but like John snr. he was a Conservative and a 'good churchman.' He took control of the business when his father retired and now his sons, John Edmond and Andrew William, were in charge. With Albert's death much of the remaining drive went out of the firm. His father was now in his eighties and took little part in the business while it is said that the sons did not have the same interest or commitment as the earlier Hayes.

During the First World War the workshops in Scotgate and West Street were put on overtime to cope with the extra orders from the Government for army carts and waggons. Two years after the war began John Hayes died, on 14 October 1916, aged ninety-four. A 'Conservative of the old school,' he took a great interest in local matters. He served on the Borough Council from 1876 to 1913, being twice Mayor, in 1882 and 1893. He was an Alderman and a Magistrate and had been Chairman of the Stamford Conservative Club. To his workmen he was a strict, but fair, employer. They called him 'Stumpy' (but not in his hearing) because he had lost a finger in a circular saw accident. Most of his men attended his funeral, the senior men acting as bearers of the coffin made in his own works from timber he had himself selected (see plates 8 and 14.)

In eighty years he had seen the family firm grow from a simple wheelwright's shop into an internationally-known firm of coach and carriage builders with a reputation for high quality products. In recent years he had also seen the change to motor powered vehicles and the challenge they brought. It was a challenge the firm had been unable or unwilling to meet. He did not, however, see the final sad end of the family firm.

In the early hours of Sunday, 31 July 1921, Ted Dexter, Hayes' works foreman, looked out of his bedroom window and saw that the West Street workshops were on fire. He raised the alarm and twenty members of the Volunteer Fire Brigade turned out. A strong wind rapidly spread the blaze which soon enveloped the whole of the body building shop at the rear of the showroom. The effect of the Brigade was 'scarcely noticeable.' The pantile roof soon collapsed and with large quantities of coal, timber and other inflammable material to feed on the fire began to get out of control. In the almshouses next door the residents prepared to move out. The firemen gave up trying to save the building and concentrated on containing the fire which was finally brought under control after several hours. Nothing was left of the body shop except the four walls and the tall chimney. The contents, which included eight large motor van bodies, several trade vehicles ready for the paint shop and an oil delivery tank, were all destroyed. Band and circular saws, planing and morticing machines and the tool kits of the twenty men employed in the shop were all lost. Some of the men had to be laid off.

The cause of the fire was a mystery. The firm had closed at 12.30pm the previous day for a four day August Holiday and a check had been made to ensure that all fires had been drawn. There was no question of defective lighting as the only illumination came from skylights. As after all major fires at business premises there was rumour and speculation circulating the town regarding the incident. An investigation by the insurers showed that because of the nature of the materials in the shop spontaneous combustion could not be ruled out. The actual cause was never discovered and in due course the insurance claim was paid.[20]

In spite of their problems Hayes and Son offered to buy the land they had been leasing in West Street since the 1860s. Early in 1922 the Trustees of the Stamford United Municipal Charities (the owners of the land) commissioned a survey and valuation of the property. The report states that the area comprised "a Stone-built and slated Office formerly a cottage, a Stone-built and tiled Wheelwright's Shop, Stone-built Stores and Tyre Furnace with corrugated roof. Brick-built and blue slated Machine shop, Stone and brick-built and tiled Blacksmith's shop, and formerly a Machine and Wheelwright's shop (158ft x 36ft) Stone-built and Blue Slated which was recently completely destroyed by fire."

The report goes on to say that the property was held on a repairing lease at a current premium of forty pounds per year; thus the lessees were liable for the reinstatement of the destroyed building. Hayes and Son's offer of £1000 was accepted and soon a new office block was erected on the site.[21]

It can only be surmised what thoughts were behind such a step. Perhaps it was felt that the investment would bring a useful return in the event of closure. If so such expectations would be disappointed. It is doubtful that fire was a direct reason for the final closure of the firm, but three years later, in 1924, Hayes and Son ceased trading. There are a number of possible explanations for the close down. The lack of interest shown by John Hayes' grandsons has already been suggested; it may be that they did not have either the commercial drive or the managerial skills to cope with running the firm during the nineteen twenties economic slump. There may have been financial reasons which are not now known. Another possible reason is the geographical location of the firm. Being in a small country town on the very edge of the East Midlands, away from the main centre of the new motor industry, may not have been the best place from which to compete with better situated coachbuilders who were able to take advantage of the growing demand from the more affluent areas of the country for motor cars. It may be significant that the Pick Motor Company, also based in Stamford, closed down the following year.

The first lot to go under the hammer at the Crown Hotel on 13 June was the West Street premises. The whole site, including the blacksmith's shop, machine shop and the new offices, and with a right of way to St Peter's Street, was sold to George Wheatley. Wheatley, who owned a large livery at the Crown and Woolpack in Scotgate, paid just £800. The site later became one of BXL Cascelloids plastics factories and is now a housing development (see plate 16.)

The following Tuesday the stocks of timber were auctioned at the Scotgate works. The quantities were impressive and give an idea of just some of the materials used in carriage and waggon building. There were 4000 cu ft dry ash planks, 800 cu ft dry oak planks, 600 cu ft dry elm planks, 7000 cu ft mahogany, white wood and pine, 2500 sawn oak spokes, 8500 ash felloes, elm and oak hubs, boards and firewood. Next

25

day the machinery was sold, planing and boring machines, spoke lathes and morticing machines and a 16hp beam engine. Several vehicles were also included in the sale, showing that production continued until the end. One of the last jobs was the construction of a motor bus body for H. Patch's new Cream Bus service which he started in 1924.

A month later the final act was played out. On 16 July the Scotgate Works themselves were sold. The blacksmiths' and wheelwrights' shop at the rear went to separate buyers; the showrooms fronting on to Scotgate were purchased by Stamford Borough for £1,750. It was proposed to convert the building into new headquarters for the town's Fire Brigade. For many years the old Newgates station had suffered from overcrowding, particularly since the purchase of a new motor tender. The escape and the hose cart were kept in sheds some distance away. The purchase of the Hayes building was to be a 'well advised step' and by May 1925 the Brigade were said to be well satisfied with their new home and remained so for the next forty years. Then on 12 February 1965 they moved into new purpose built headquarters in Radcliffe Road. Two years later, in May 1967, Hayes' Scotgate showroom was demolished. Only the flag pole and the yard gates, made from a pair of iron wheels, were saved to be re-erected at the new fire station.[22]

Conclusion

There are many aspects of Hayes and Son's history which have not been examined and many questions about their activities still to be answered. This is because so much of the information necessary has either been lost or is not available. Nothing remains of the firm's business or administrative papers and so questions about production or finances, about employment figures or wages, cannot be answered. There is little documentary evidence of any kind and other source material is sparse. Even the surviving members of the family have little knowledge of the business.

The numbers of employees must at times have been quite high considering the quantity of vehicles produced, but the only figure we have comes from the 1871 Census which shows that John Hayes employed twenty-nine men and seven boys. From a handful of apprenticeship indentures which survive in the Stamford Town Hall archives we can get an idea of the wages of these boys. Before the First World War apprentices started at five shillings a week, rising after four years to ten shillings a week. According to the daughter of a former Hayes coach painter the average wage for a skilled workman at that time was one pound a week.

Few people in Stamford can now remember the old firm. Those who do still call West Street 'Hayes' Hill.' One can recall the excitement of the 1921 fire; another remembers the works' foreman ringing the dinner bell for the hour break; another the works' football team in black shorts and white shirts with a blue cartwheel on the breast pocket.

When these memories are lost all that will remain of this fine firm will be a few vehicles and a pair of iron gates.

Notes and Sources

1. Hayes and Son Catalogue 1880. An incomplete copy is in the Phillips' Collection, Stamford Town Hall. Among the many testimonials quoted is the following:

"Wombwell's Menagerie, Tradegar.

Messrs Hayes and Son, Stamford.

Dear Sirs,

I have much pleasure in informing you that the new Rhinoceros Waggon has given general satisfaction. I consider it is the master-piece of workmanship as regards lightness, durability, and neatness. I hope you are pushing on with my other orders as fast as possible.

I am dear Sirs, yours truly,   J. C. Edmonds."

2. *Inventory of The Town of Stamford*, Royal Commission on Historic Monuments, 1977, p. lxxxvi; p. 74.

3. *Lincoln Rutland and Stamford Mercury* (LRSM) 20 October 1854.

4. The Royal Agricultural Society of England (RASE) journals and catalogues have provided much of the information relating to Hayes' at RASE exhibitions.

5. LRSM 16 December 1859; 28 June 1861.

6. LRSM 20 March 1866; mortgage deed 6 September 1873 restating conveyance

7 April 1866, from Richard Hillier, Peterborough Library.

7. LRSM 24 September 1869.

8. LRSM 17 December 1897.

9. LRSM 10 July 1870.

10. LRSM 3 April 1874.

11. History of Rock Iron Works taken from a bundle of conveyances and other documents relating to the site formerly held in Stamford Town Hall but now believed to be somewhere in the South Kesteven District Council archives at Grantham.

12. *London Post Office Directories* 1884, 1892, and *Carriage Builders Journal*, 1902.

13. See Appendix 2.

14. Lincolnshire Agricultural Society catalogues; LRSM 20 October 1916.

15. LRSM 17 December 1897.

16. *London Post Office Directories* 1902, 1903.

17. LRSM 13 November 1903. After his death J. E. Hayes' business is believed to have been moved to Hoxton in north London by his son Arthur. There he produced milk floats and other small trade vehicles. The firm was taken over by a large concern about 1914 and it lost its corporate identity. Another of J. E. Hayes' sons, William, took over the carriage building firm of W. Bennet of Launceston Road, Callington, Cornwall, *c.*1913 (Kelly's Cornwall Directory 1914). He closed the works down at the end of 1916 when his men were called into the army. He then left the trade and became a commercial traveller. He died in 1969.

18. LRSM 23 Oct 1902; scrapbook of news cuttings in Stamford Museum.

19. *Carriage and Wheelwrights Journal* 1903, 1904, 1905

20. LRSM 5 Aug 1921.

21. Reports and Conveyances in Charities Chest, Stamford Town Hall.

22. LRSM 6 June 1924; 15 May 1925; 14 May 1954; 5 May 1967.

Appendix one
Known Stamford Employees

Fred Baxter.	Coach painter in 1920.
Frederick Cave.	Wheelwright apprentice 1893.
- Cooper.	Accident in 1903.
"Billy" Cozens.	Went to Derby when firm closed down. Died 1934.
Walter Beaumont.	Coachmaker, apprenticed 1901, went first to Humber of Coventry then to Hollick and Pratt as body designer, taken over by Morris, died 1932.
William Blake.	Apprenticed 1862.
John Evan Davies.	Apprenticed coach bodymaker 1913.
Edward [Ted] Dexter.	Works foreman 1921.
Thomas Jackson Dexter.	Wheelwright in 1921, died 1923.
- Fenn.	Coach painter *c.*1920.
John Flint.	Cleaner in 1900 accident.
- Haddon.	Wheelwright.
Arthur Brinsley Haylock.	Apprenticed motor body builder 1920, he was probably Hayes' last apprentice; the firm closed down four years later.
- Humberstone.	Wheelwright.
John Henry Jennings.	Apprenticed coach smith 1911.
Ted Johnson.	
Edward[?] Joyce.	Wheelwright, apprenticed *c.*1896.
- Lang.	Coach painter *c.*1920.
Frank Lound.	Coach painter *c.*1920.
Horace Young Nutt.	Apprenticed *c.*1875, Became head of Barkers the Royal carriage builders, died during WW2 aged about 80.
- Pickett.	Foreman of carriage builder's shop, 1894.
- Piggott.	Coach painter.
Joseph Reedman.	Head Clerk 1883 to 1923, retired November 1923, died December 1923 aged 77.
John Thomas Rippey.	Apprenticed 1885.
Arthur Noel Roffe.	Apprenticed coach bodymaker 1914.
William Olphin Rouse.	Apprenticed 1858.
- Sambridge.	When firm closed down went into partnership with Wakefield as wheelwrights in Empingham Road.

29

Benjamin Scotney.	Apprenticed 1870.
- Semmence.	Wheelwright apprentice.
John Thomas Simpson.	Apprenticed 1868.
Alfred William Tiddy.	Apprenticed coach bodymaker 1912.
William Tofield.	Foreman of wheelwrights' shop, 1894.
Henry Towell.	Apprenticed 1866.
- Uff.	Painter injured in 1897.
- Wakefield	*See* Sambridge, *above.*
- Wainwright.	Coach painter *c.*1920.
Henry Webster.	Apprenticed 1879.
Thomas Winterton jnr.	Apprenticed 1865.

Sources

References to Hayes' employees are few. The occasional report in the *Stamford Mercury*, usually of an accident, has provided some. Others have come from the papers of the Earl of Exeter's Apprenticing Charity and the Stamford United Municipal Charities which are to be found in the Stamford Town Hall archives. The remainder are from conversations with people who had relations working for the firm.

Appendix Two

Shows attended by Hayes and Son

Abbreviations

R.A.S.E. Royal Agricultural Society of England.

N.A.S. Northamptonshire Agricultural Society.

N.L.A.S. North Lincolnshire Agricultural Society.

L.A.S. Lincolnshire Agricultural Society.

1855 R.A.S.E. Carlisle.	1865 R.A.S.E. Plymouth.
1856 R.A.S.E. Chelmsford.	1865 N.A.S. Peterborough.
1857 R.A.S.E. Salisbury.	1865 N.L.A.S. Rasen (Lincs).
1858 R.A.S.E. Chester.	1867 R.A.S.E. Bury St. Edmunds.
1859 R.A.S.E. Warwick.	1867 Paris Exhibition.
1860 R.A.S.E. Canterbury.	1867 N.A.S. Towcester.
1861 R.A.S.E. Leeds.	1868 R.A.S.E. Leicester.
1862 R.A.S.E. Battersea.	1869 R.A.S.E. Manchester.
1863 R.A.S.E. Worcester.	1869 L.A.S. Lincoln.
1864 R.A.S.E. Newcastle.	1870 L.A.S. Sleaford

1871 R.A.S.E. Wolverhampton.
1871 L.A.S. Brigg.
1872 R.A.S.E. Cardiff.
1872 L.A.S. Spalding.
1873 R.A.S.E. Hull.
1873 L.A.S. Gainsborough.
1874 R.A.S.E. Bedford.
1874 L.A.S. Grantham.
1875 R.A.S.E. Taunton.
1875 L.A.S. Grimsby.
1875 N.A.S. Stamford.
1876 R.A.S.E. Birmingham.
1876 R.A.S.E. Liverpool.
1878 R.A.S.E. Bristol.
1878 Paris Exhibition.
1879 R.A.S.E. Kilburn.
1881 R.A.S.E. Derby.
1882 R.A.S.E. Reading.
1882 L.A.S. Sleaford
1883 R.A.S.E. York.
1884 R.A.S.E. Shrewsbury.
1884 L.A.S. Grantham
1884 Dairy Show London.
1886 R.A.S.E. Norwich
1886 N.A.S. Stamford
1887 L.A.S. Spalding
1888 R.A.S.E. Nottingham.

1889 R.A.S.E. 50th show Windsor.
1890 L.A.S. Boston.
1891 R.A.S.E. Doncaster.
1892 R.A.S.E. Warwick.
1892 L.A.S. Lincoln.
1893 R.A.S.E. Chester.
1894 R.A.S.E. Cambridge.
1895 L.A.S. Spalding.
1895 R.A.S.E. Darlington.
1896 R.A.S.E. Leicester.
1897 R.A.S.E. Manchester.
1898 R.A.S.E. Birmingham.
1899 R.A.S.E. Maidstone.
1900 R.A.S.E. York.
1902 Dairy Show London.
1902 Brewers Exhibition London.
1903 R.A.S.E. Park Royal London.
1903 Dairy Show London.
1903 Peterborough Agricultural Show.
1904 R.A.S.E. Park Royal London.
1904 L.A.S. Grimsby.
1905 R.A.S.E. Park Royal London.
1905 Dairy Show London.
1906 R.A.S.E. Derby.
1907 R.A.S.E. Lincoln.
1910 Arts and Industry Exhibition,
    Stamford.

Appendix Three
Hayes and the Showmen

Through the marriage of Albert Henry Hayes in 1879 to Margaret Emma Edmonds, Hayes and Son of Stamford became associated with probably the greatest and most famous of all travelling shows: Wombwell's Menagerie. The biography of that most enterprising of gentlemen, George Wombwell, has yet to be written but until it is, this brief history will put into context the show people to whom Hayes supplied waggons and vans and to whom they were related. The pedigree (Appendix four) clarifies the family relationships.

George Wombwell was born at Duddenhoe End, near Saffron Walden, on 24 December 1777, and died aged 73, on 16 November 1850 at Northallerton, Yorkshire. He was not the first to take a collection of wild animals around the country fairs; many others had preceded him, but his Menagerie was to be the greatest and the most famous. He is said to have been a Soho shoemaker who at the age of 27 bought a pair of boa constrictors for £75 which he exhibited as a sideline in a back room of his shop (Mark Sorrell suggests it was in 1807 at a shop in Piccadilly). He had soon made enough to cover the cost of his purchase and, realising both his ability in handling animals and the commercial prospects in animal shows, he began his collection and presented his first exhibition in 1808 at St James' Fair, Bristol. Two years later he appeared for the first time at Bartholomew Fair, Smithfield, London. By 1816 he had built up a large collection of animals which he took on the road in cage waggons and a living van.

By the 1820s Wombwell's Menagerie was a regular visitor to most of the major fairs around the country, presenting a large and varied collection of animals and animal acts. The first appearance at Stamford's Mid-Lent Fair was in 1819. He was a showman of some ability and quick to spot a chance of taking customers from his competitors. There is an often-told story which illustrates this. Hearing, while in Newcastle, that his greatest rival, Atkins, was advertising the only elephant at Smithfield, Wombwell set off with his entire show and force-marched to London. On arrival his elephant was found to be dead in its waggon. Atkins took this opportunity to advertise 'the only living elephant at the fair'. Wombwell countered with 'the only dead elephant at the fair' and showed it to packed houses, dead elephants being scarcer than live ones.

In the 1820s cock fighting and animal baiting were still common sports and Wombwell was not averse to making money out of them. He set up fights between his lions, Wallace and Nero, and dogs which have variously been described as mastiffs and bulldogs. At Warwick admission charges 'ranged from a guinea to five guineas and every seat was taken.' Not everyone approved. William Hone, in 1825, sharply censured Wombwell in his *Table Book* for having exposed his fine lion Nero to be baited by dogs at Warwick and displaying a disgusting picture of the fight outside his show. He described Wombwell as "undersized in mind, as well as in form, a weazen man, with a skin reddened by more than natural spirits, and he speaks in a voice and language that accords with his feelings and propensities." Henry Morley, in 1859, wrote, "of this man who began life as a cobbler in Monmouth Street, I can find only unfavourable record. He must however have had an unusual ability and energy in his peculiar way. His collection was good." Nero died in November 1827 and was sent to a Mr M. N. Shipton, a Birmingham surgeon, for dissection.

Wombwell collected animals through special port agents who watched ship arrivals and by an arrangement with the Thames pilots who told him if any incoming vessels were carrying animals so he could get first chance of buying them. Importing foreign animals was a risky business. Not only could it be costly but the lack of knowledge regarding diet and habitat could be fatal. Wombwell bought the first giraffe that was imported; he paid £1000 for it. It was taken to his Commercial Road yard but died while a special waggon was being built for it.

By 1840 Wombwell's collection had grown to be the largest, and probably the best, travelling menagerie in the country. Thomas Frost tells us that he

"had twelve lions, besides lionesses and cubs, and eight tigers, a tigress, and cubs, in addition to a puma, a jaguar, a black tiger, several leopards, an ocelot, a serval, and a pair of genets. There were also striped and spotted hyenas, wolves, jackals, coati-mondis, racoons, a polar bear, a sloth bear, black and brown bears, a honey bear, and a couple of porcupines. The hoofed classes were represented by three elephants, a fine one-horned rhinoceros, a pair of gnus, a white antelope, a brahmin cow, an axis deer, and three giraffes - the first of their kind ever exhibited at the fair."

Feeding such a variety of animals as Wombwell travelled must have been a prodigious task. The lions and tigers were each fed twelve pounds of meat each day, the bears only had meat in the winter but for the rest of the year were fed on bread, biscuit and boiled rice. The elephants, camels, antelopes and the dozens of horses used to haul the cage waggons and living vans consumed an enormous quantity of hay, cabbages, boiled rice and bread.

Of all Wombwell's animals and freaks his elephants feature in many of the stories about the man and his menageries (he eventually operated three); the earliest, of course, being the 'only dead elephant at the fair.' Another tells of the elephant which escaped from its stable one night in Croydon and broke into a baker's shop and ate sixteen four-pound loaves and was about to start on the sweets jars when it was recaptured. In 1862, long after Wombwell was dead, it was a Wombwell elephant, parading through the streets of Leicester, between whose feet a young, pregnant, crippled girl stumbled and fell. Her name was Mary Jane Merrick, her son was Joseph Carey Merrick whose facial deformities were to earn him the name 'Elephant Man.'

Excitement of a different kind was provided by the carnivores. On a visit to Stamford's Mid-Lent Fair in 1842, a local farmer was seized by one of the tigers, fixing its teeth into his fore-arm and attempting to drag him into the cage. All attempts to release him failed: the animal would only let go when a hot iron was applied to its nose. The man had been drinking and had ignored repeated warnings that teasing the tiger was 'foolish and dangerous.' No blame was attached to Wombwell or his assistants, the safety arrangements were reported to be excellent.

Wombwell's menagerie appeared before royalty on several occasions. The first time was at Thirsk in 1830 before the young Princess Victoria; then four years later in front of King William IV and Queen Adelaide. There was also an appearance in Windsor Castle Quadrangle before Queen Victoria and Prince Albert in 1847 from which event the title 'Royal Windsor Castle Menagerie' was coined. A second appearance at Windsor Castle took place in 1854 and there was a final appearance before royalty at Ballater in 1869.

By the time he died in 1850, Wombwell was operating three menageries. His first, founded in 1808, was the biggest and the best. The others, number two dating from 1842, and number three acquired from a showman called Morgan, who died c.1831, were much smaller affairs. Wombwell was buried in Highgate Cemetery, London, in an oak coffin made by one of his musicians from timbers of the warship 'Royal George' which he had carried with him for many years. Under the terms of his will the number one menagerie was left to his widow, Ann. She operated it until her retirement in 1866 when it was taken over by Alexander

Fairgrieve who had married a niece of Wombwell's, Harriet Blight. It was to this menagerie and show that Hayes and Son of Stamford supplied several waggons and a 'Velocipede Circus.' This ride was perhaps an attempt to bring life into the show, which seems to have been in decline. In the event the menagerie was sold in 1872 by auction at Edinburgh. The number three menagerie was left to a nephew, George Wombwell junior. He was the son of Wombell's brother Zachariah. It too was disposed of by auction, in 1855. Only the number two menagerie survived.

The number two menagerie was left to another niece, Harriet Edmonds, a daughter of George's brother, William, and wife of James Edmonds. Harriet had worked for Wombwell as an animal trainer. Under her management the number two menagerie became the successor to the great tradition of Wombwell's menageries. She claimed that not only was it the largest menagerie, but it "had the greatest number of specimens, greatest variety and the most beautiful groups of trained lions, panthers, leopards and tigers." Mrs Edmonds carried on until 1884 when it was taken over by her son James who sold it to Edward Henry Bostock. Her youngest daughter Margaret Emma married Albert Henry Hayes.

Edward Henry Bostock was a son of James Bostock II and Emma Wombwell, Harriet's sister. He joined his father's menagerie when he was 12 and left in 1883 to start his own show, buying Edmonds' menagerie in 1884. In 1889 he bought his mother's and later acquired his brother Frank's show.

James Bostock II was born at Dairy House Farm, Leek. He was a son of James Bostock of Barnslea, Staffordshire, a wealthy farmer and landowner, and Mary Wardle. At the age of 24 he got a job as a waggoner in Wombwell's (later Edmonds') menagerie. Ten years later he was the contracting and advertising agent; it was he who obtained the royal commands to exhibit the menagerie at Windsor in 1847 and 1854. In 1852 he married Emma, daughter of William and Hannah Wombwell, at Tollesbury, Essex. He left Harriet Edmonds' employ in 1867 and set up his own travelling menagerie. James Bostock died on 12 April 1878 at Farnham, Surrey and was buried at Leek Cemetery, leaving the menagerie to his widow.

The combination of the Bostocks' shows around the nucleus formed by Wombwell's number two menagerie led to the famous title appearing on show fronts and steam engine canopies for the first time in 1889: 'BOSTOCK AND WOMBWELL'S MENAGERIE.'

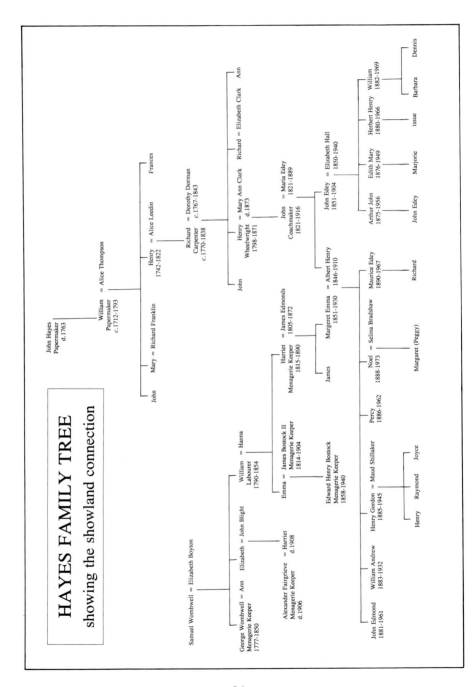

HAYES FAMILY TREE
showing the showland connection

John Hayes
Papermaker
d.1763

William = Alice Thompson
Papermaker
c.1712-1793

Mary = Richard Franklin

John

Henry = Alice Leedin
1742-1822

Frances

Richard = Dorothy Dorman
Carpenter   c.1767-1843
c.1770-1838

John

Henry = Mary Ann Clark
Wheelwright   d.1873
1798-1871

Richard = Elizabeth Clark   Ann

John = Maria Edey
Coachmaker   1821-1889
1821-1916

John Edey = Elizabeth Hall
1851-1904   1850-1940

Albert Henry
1846-1910

Margaret Emma
1851-1930

Arthur John
1875-1956

John Edey

Edith Mary
1876-1949

Marjorie

Herbert Henry
1880-1966

issue

William
1882-1969

Barbara

Dennis

Samuel Wombwell = Elizabeth Boyton

George Wombwell = Ann
Menagerie Keeper
1777-1850

Elizabeth = John Blight

William = Hanna
Labourer
1790-1854

Emma = James Bostock II
Menagerie Keeper
1814-1904

Harriet = James Edmonds
Menagerie Keeper   1805-1872
1815-1890

James

Alexander Fairgrieve = Harriet
Menagerie Keeper   d.1908
d.1906

Edward Henry Bostock
Menagerie Keeper
1858-1940

Maurice Edey
1890-1967

Richard

Noel = Selina Bradshaw
1888-1973

Margaret (Peggy)

Percy
1886-1962

Henry Gordon = Maud Shillaker
1885-1945

Henry   Raymond   Joyce

William Andrew
1883-1932

John Edmond
1881-1961

36

Sources

Morley, Henry, *Memoirs of Bartholomew Fair* (1859).

Frost, Thomas, *The Old Showmen and the London Fairs* (1874).

Altick, Richard, *Shows of London* (1978).

Beaver, Patrick,*The Spice of Life* (1979).

Middlemiss, John, *A Zoo On Wheels* (1987).

The Stamford and Rutland Mercury (1819, 1827, 1842, 1884).

I am also indebted to Mark Sorrell for giving me access to his research into the life of George Wombwell and his Menageries.

Appendix Four
Other Coachmakers in Stamford

Stamford, situated as it is astride the Great North Road and serving a rich agricultural hinterland, was a centre for a number of coachmakers and wheelwrights who produced carriages for the gentry and carts and waggons for the farmers. Some appeared only fleetingly, others flourished with successful businesses. The sources for them all are often fragmentary and scattered. The following is a handlist of those found so far among the pages of the *Stamford and Rutland Mercury* (SM), Town Directories, Parish Registers, the Borough Minute Books (HB, for Hall Books) and Freemen's Minute Books (FB). It does not claim to be complete, but rather to be a starting point for further research.

BARTON:

William Barton, coachmaker, with Edward Taylor, harnessmaker, has left John Young, of St Martins - enquiries for their services of Francis Freeman's, The Swan and Woolpocket in St Martins. SM 6 September 1716.

BERRIDGE:

Anthony Berridge, wheelwright, Stamford Baron. SM 9 October 1801. To be sold by auction at the premises of Mr A Berridge, the Waggon and Horses Inn, St Martin's, Stamford Baron; An elegant four-wheeled travelling carriage, the late property of the greatest of all great men. [A reference to Daniel Lambert, England's fattest man, who died in the Waggon and Horses the previous year.] SM 19 October 1810.

Anthony Berridge, wheelwright, buried St Martins. 10 December 1812.

Anthony Berridge, landlord of the Waggon and Horses died aged 50. SM 11 December 1812.

Elizabeth Berridge, widow of Anthony Berridge, to carry on wheelwrighting and innkeeping. SM 28 Aug 1812.

Anthony Berridge's wheelwright shop to let, apply Elizabeth Berridge. SM 26 Oct 1821.

Elizabeth Berridge buried St Martins. 13 May 1824.

Mrs Berridge of Waggon and Horses died aged 52. SM 14 May 1824.

BROWNING:

John Browning, wheelwright, purchased his freedom of the Borough of Stamford for £6.13s.4d. in 1734. HB p76.

To be sold at John Browning's in St Martins, Stamford Baron, two second-hand Chariots, a new Four-wheel'd Chaise, and an old one. NB.

All sorts of Coachmaker's and Harnessmaker's work is elegantly perform'd by John Browning aforesaid. SM 25 March 1736.

John Browning, coachmaker in Stamford Baron. SM 8 September 1737.

Mr John Browning buried 21 November 1744 St Martins.

Jn Browning dec. coachmaker and wheelwright, late tenant of very good, convenient dwelling house in Stamford Baron with commodious and well accustomed shop adjoining to be let. Stock of wood etc. Enquire Mrs Browning or Mr Arch of St Martins. SM 19 April 1744.

Mrs Constance Browning, widow, buried 21 January 1746 St Martins.

CLOW:

Benjamin Price Clow first appears in Stamford as a springmaker on the north-west corner of Scotgate and West St in 1879. Jenkinson's Almanack, Kelly's Directory.

Advertises regularly in Dolby's Directories until 1915.

GUNTON:

Gunton and Son, Castle Hill Carriage Works. Dolby's Directories 1898 to 1910.

HIBBINS and PAINE:

John Hibbins and Thomas Paine [former coachmakers employed by Robertsons] take over Robertson's coach works. SM 20 December 1872.

"A magnificent state carriage for the Marquis of Exeter has just been turned out of the atelier of Messrs Hibbins and Payne, carriage builders, St Martins. The Burghley arms and the coronet are emblazoned on a rich shell-blue ground, most delicately painted, and the hammer-cloth is of elaborate workmanship. The whole is indeed a work of art reflecting credit upon the town as well as the firm who have executed the order." SM 24 April 1874.

HUTCHINGS:

See Robertson.

LAXTON:

John Laxton selling Chariot. SM 15 May 1718, 15 August 1723, 19 September 1723.

LITTLER:

Stephen Litteller [sic], coachmaker, purchased his freedom of the Borough of Stamford for £10 in 1716. HB p290.

Stephen Littler in St Mary's Street, Stamford, for coachwork and painting. SM 16 May 1717.

Chariot and Chaise to be let or sold at Mr Littler's, a coachmaker from London, in St Marys Street. Note, Mr Littler never worked with Mr Young in St Martins. SM 25 July 1717.

NEALE:

.... Neale, coachmaker, in St Martins. SM 28 May 1772.

.... Neale, coachmaker, in Stamford Baron. SM 2 June 1774.

William Neale has taken over Henry Tyler's coachmaking business in St Martins. SM 5 October 1775.

Wm Neale, coachmaker, St Martins, Stamford Baron. SM 8 May 1777.

Wm Neale, coachmaker of St Martins, deceased, sale of his goods. SM 12 August 1779.

Mrs Neale, coachmaker in St Martins. SM 6 May 1785.

R Turtle, coach and harnessmaker at late Mr Neale's shop in St Martins. SM 30 March 1787.

NEVILLE:

John Neville, wheelwright, purchased his freedom of the Borough of Stamford for £8 in 1766. HB p312.

John Neville and Rich Taylor advertise for late Henry Tyler's trade. To carry on coachmaking in St Marys Street. Both employed by Henry Tyler for over 20 years. SM 5 October 1775.

Jn Neville dissolves partnership with Rich Taylor, to continue the trade. SM 20 June 1776.

ROBERTSON:

John Robertson, coachmaker, dissolves partnership with Joseph Hutchings, Robertson to continue the business in St Marys Street. SM 2 September 1786.

J. Robertson, coachmaker, St Marys Street. SM March 1788.

J. Robertson, coachmaker of Stamford, selling post chaise and coach. SM 29 October 1790.

Advertises regularly in *Stamford Mercury*.

William and Charles James Robertson, coachbuilders, St Martins. White's *Directory* 1842 and 1859.

Miss Mary Robertson, coachbuilder, 23 High Street, St Martins. White's *Directory* 1872.

John Hibbins and Thomas Paine take over Robertson's coachworks. LRSM 20 December 1872.

SPENCER:

John Spencer. Mourning coach for hire in Stamford. SM 15 March 1716/17.

William Spencer, wheelwright, purchased his freedom of the Borough of Stamford for £8 in August 1821. FB.

Charles Francis Spencer, coachmaker, took up his freedom of the Borough by birthright, being the son of a freeman, 9 October 1834. FB.

Charles Francis Spencer died April 1841 aged 29. St Michael's memorial.

William Spencer died aged 74. SM 2 March 1860.

Carriage Manufactory, High St., Stamford, Miss M.A.Spencer, having disposed of her business to Messrs Hayes and Son of Stamford and Peterboro' begs most respectfully... *etc*. SM 24 September 1869.

TAYLOR:

Edward Taylor, *see* William Barton.

Richard Taylor, wheelwright, took up his freedom of the Borough, being the son of freeman Richard Taylor, victualler, in 1743. HB p127.

Rich Taylor, *see* John Neville.

TURTLE:

R. Turtle, coach and harnessmaker, at late Mr Neale's shop in St Martins. SM 30 March 1787.

Mr Turtle at the Bull and Swan, St Martins. SM 2 Nov 1787.

R. Turtle, coach and harnessmaker, St Martins. SM 25 April 1788.

R. Turtle son of the late Mr Turtle is continuing the Bull and Swan and malting business, Mrs Turtle continuing coachmaking business. SM 10 August 1792.

Sarah, wife of Richard Turtle, gentleman, buried 23 June 1809, aged 35, St Martins. [Widow of William Neale, coachmaker, she married Richard Turtle, himself a widower, on 14 September 1786 in St Martins.]

Richard Turtle, formerly eminent coach proprietor, died aged 53. SM 2 February 1821.

TYLER:

Henry Tyler, wheelwright, purchased his freedom of the Borough of Stamford for £6.13s.4d. in 1719. HB p303.

Henry Tyler coachmaker in the Beast Market, Stamford. SM 15 Oct 1724.

William Banister apprenticed to Henry Tyler, coachmaker, by indenture dated 6 November 1728. HB p49.

Henry Tyler, coachmaker. For sale a very good coach, 2 Chariots and a four-wheel'd chaise, in Stamford. SM 8 June 1738.

Henry Tyler, coachmaker. For sale light machine Chariot, lined with green cloth. SM 20 March 1739/40.

Henry Tyler, nephew and successor to late Mr Henry Tyler, coachmaker, of St Martins, Stamford Baron is continuing the business at the same shop. SM 30 March 1775.

Henry Tyler's coachmaking business in St Martins taken over by William Neale. SM 5 October 1775.

YOUNG:

William Barton, coachmaker, and Edward Taylor, harnessmaker, have left John Young, wheelwright, in St Martins. SM 6 September 1716.

John Young, coachmaker in St Martins. For sale Coach and Chariot, also Timber for sale. It lies by the Stamford Navigable River for convenience of sending away. SM 7 February 1716/17.

John Young. Coaches and Chaises to be Sold in St Martins. SM 13 June 1717.

Mr Littler never worked with Mr Young in St Martins. SM 25 July 1717.

Other local titles from Paul Watkins

DUCKMANTON, CAROLYN, *Exploring Cambridgeshire Churches.* A delightful popular guide to the churches of Cambridgeshire, lavishly illustrated by Anthony Sursham (early 1991).

GUNTON, SYMON, *The History of the Church of Peterborough*, reprinted for the first time since 1686. Gunton's work was the pioneer history of Peterborough and has long since been regarded as a classic. It has been reissued with a new and comprehensive index by Anne Wilkins and a modern introductory essay by Canon Higham of Peterborough Cathedral. *Price £28*

HILL, SIR FRANCIS, *Medieval Lincoln.* A reprint of Hill's definitive history of medieval Lincoln with a modern essay by Dr. Dorothy Owen. Paperback, 524 pages, *price £14.95*

MAHANY, CHRISTINE, *Stamford Castle and Town.* A general account of Stamford's archaeology (early 1991).

SMITH, MARTIN, *Walks Through Four Counties, Country Walks from Central Stamford.* A walking guide for the Stamford area, packed with illustrations, maps and historical information. Thirty two pages, *price £1.95*

SMITH, MARTIN, *Stamford Myths and Legends.* A fascinating and original study of Stamford's folklore. Includes accounts of Stamford's ancient university, Roger Bacon's brazen head, miracles and ghost tales, the Stamford bull-running and curious people, such as Daniel Lambert. Contains many illustrations by the author (early 1991).

SMITH, MARTIN, *Stamford Then and Now.* A detailed examination of Stamford's changing townscape. The author uses drawings based on old photographs and prints to reconstruct buildings that have since been demolished or altered. It provides a valuable record of Stamford's vanished past (early 1991).

WHEELER, WILLIAM HENRY, *The History of the Fens of South Lincolnshire.* A reprint of this classic and scarce late nineteenth century fenland history with an introductory essay by Brian Simmons of the Trust for Lincolnshire Archaeology. *Price £30*